Cimarrón

THE WESLEYAN POETRY PROGRAM : VOLUME 94

Cimarrón

Poems by
RICARDO ALONSO

Wesleyan University Press
MIDDLETOWN, CONNECTICUT

Grateful acknowledgement is made to the following publications, in which some of these poems have appeared: *Areito, Broadside, The Greenfield Review, Joven Cuba, Obsidian, Praxis, West End.*

"Poor Boy Number Two" from *Wake Up, Dead Man: Afro-American Work-songs from Texas Prisons,* by Bruce Jackson, 1972, quoted with permission of Harvard University Press.

The publisher gratefully acknowledges support of the publication of this book by the Andrew W. Mellon Foundation.

Manufactured in the United States of America
First edition

For Myrta

Contents

Arriving Logan from San Juan   11

Summer Evening / Mission Hill   14

Winos   19

Caribe Blue   20

Escapee's Blues   23

CJ   24

News Item   25

America is a Junkie   28

For Langston Hughes   30

Bluesman   31

Rain   32

Cornell Roosevelt Thomas   35

Brujería   36

Project Lovesong   37

Some Call it Home	38
Five Songs for Puerto Rico	40
Abuela y Patria	45
Tiempo Muerto	46
Aguacero	48
Songs for Puerto Rico #2	49
Canto Popular	52
Afro Blue	55
Song of the Drum	56
Rumba	58
Changó / Thunder	63
Rumba Fragments	64
Dance of the Ancestors	66
Cimarrón	69
Morning Coming	71

Cimarrón

Arriving Logan from San Juan

tourists:
eager pink flesh
dyed smiling brown
and you
jíbaro
hesitant in the back
stiffening to the first breath
of cold
a few hours ago
you were there

you bring
island food cooked this morning
island fruit picked yesterday
island soil fresh in your nails
answer
(is the field still there
did they knock down the house)
questions

you look
for old faces

Papi
source of the mountain
stream
my father
how long will it be
long will it be
till they have you

jíbaro: a peasant farmer of Puerto Rico. Taino name meaning "free."

pica pica picoteando
a pigeon scrambling for puke
off a hot pavement

and you Grandmother
abuelita mía
old lady of many languages
beware the cold cold cold
that no suéter can keep out
curse that no saint
can cure
that last winter
killed my santa
split her in two
and left her
for the winos to piss on
cuídate Abuelita

and Dalia
welcome to la vida
(en inglis)
to los hombres and los celos and los hijos
and los hombres and las noches solas
and los hijos and el cheque and la ropa
and la comida
de lata
mucha lata
yours will be a special pain
brown eyes blinded
by a gray world
a sweet bolero
drowning in the desert

island food
cooked this morning
island fruit
picked yesterday
island soil
brown smelling

jíbaro	jíbaro
desembarcas	you land
con tu salsa	with your rhythm
con tu alma	with your soul
de palmera recta	of straight palm
con tu salsa	with your rhythm
con tu corazón	with your heart
de tierra tibia	of warm earth
con tu salsa	with your rhythm

jíbaro
jíbarooo
jíbaro dont stay
go away dont
dont stay jíbaro
no te quedes jíbaro
dont stay dont dont stay dont
go away vete lejos
dont stay jíbaro
jíbaro go away
doooonnnnt

jíbaro

Summer Evening/Mission Hill

Summer evening
and rhythms sighing
in and out of broken windows
guaguancó and soft sones
uneasy
in this strange place
Summer evening
and the street hums
the hazy pace
of the teenagers' stroll
long street
and downtown buildings blinking
on a summer evening
far away

Summer evening
and he stands
slick as sweat
by the Parker St. Lounge
stands
smooth as the shine
of his '74 Lincoln
a stick
or a bag
of anything you'd care to buy
Summer evening
slick as sweat
a bitch
for every taste
he

guaguancó: dance rhythm of Cuban origin; up tempo, fast-paced.
son: style of Cuban music, country cousin of the cha-cha.

slick as sweat
summer evening
grinning on the corner

And Chino thinks
maybe this time
his rap has worked
on the Irish girl
hushed laughter
and later
will she
go up
on the roof

And Marta
sitting on a rust colored stoop
in the blood colored light
knows that she knew then
before she came
she was going to lose out
in the end
She stops to scold
a girl child
And she knows well
not to ask
will he be here tomorrow

Summer evening
and they hang in groups
around their cars
sweetness of music
and reefer
Repressed rhythm
on a summer evening

15

Can you walk around
all day
with your guts slowly falling open
Nobody screams
until they go crazy
It just isn't cool
(The death colored walls
of the state prison
wait for you
and the four strands
of electric wire
will be your only horizon)
There are days
I wake up wanting to cry
decide to get high
and stare at TV
(The tall white walls
of the state prison
reach for you
yearn silently
for the night
you slip off the tightrope
the night
you shatter like a streetlamp
ten thousand jagged pieces
of a jagged dream)

Summer evening
and he works his guitar
slowly
struggling to remember
the sound of night
mountain rivers
and coquí songs

of childhood with fresh grass
Summer evening
and his guitar
slowly struggling to remember
the way into
the summer night

The old lady
is
dry boned
loose skinned
her apartment quiet
walls hung
with pictures of the warriors
and bunches of dark bananas
Young mothers
come to her
'Mi'ja yo no ayudo a nadie'
But my baby is sick
'Child I don't help anyone'
And in her last days
she chants alone
and calls destruction
on project cages
dreams of lime
in gringo eyes
poison spears
in gringo dreams
Her two large dogs
growl
at any breath on the outside
and her children

coquí: a small tree frog, found only in Puerto Rico. Its name is a song, which it
repeats in the night.

and grandchildren
stay away

Summer evening and no
my number didn't
come out this week
and I
must be going
crazy
because today
it really matters

Summer evening
into summer night
and I hide
deep inside you
the cage is gone
our eyes are shut
there are no words
we are on the beach
and the smell of your skin
everywhere

Winos

Three in winter
broken angels
saying I love you

Caribe Blue

(for P. R.)

sueña con ella
sueña
dream in island colors
sueña

Exiles:

small girl swings
sky leaps from playground dirt
face to the sky
skirt in the wind
swings

woman
color of a country moon
kneeling in an empty church
old man
prays drunken
to pigeons in the park
his wife screaming
for a match
from a bench
we
buy lottery tickets
and wait

give me water
I am a prisoner
I want to drink

in an abandoned building
they shot each other
blood among burnt mattresses
she was left frozen
they sent the bodies back
on the same plane

are we
to dance forever
on broken glass
sueña con ella
that you'll be alive
vivo

sueña con ella
in the heat of dance
sueña
in the cool of dance
sueña
when the street
is closing in
sueña
the first time
you see your child . . .
when your old lady dies
sueña

prisoner
exile
fool
dreamer

soñador

Hey
we are the juice of the rainbow
the palm trees pray
for our return

Escapee's Blues

Prison air is cradled in deafness
suckled by iron bars
The breath of screws
and their ancestors

Freedom is a fire
Freedom is a wound
burst open
no stitches will hold it
no cotton smother the flesh
screaming

"Just one more chance in a life
            to do the right or wrong
This hell won't be my potion no
            this hell won't be my home
This hell won't be my home boy
            won't be my home
Just one more chance in a life
            to do the right or wrong"

He asked for bread
they gave him none
he asked for fish
they have him a bone
to stick in his throat
and finish his song

"Just one more chance . . ." based on "Poor Boy Number Two," a ballad by J. B. Smith.

23

CJ

The youngest wrist
with digital watch
The rest look
and wish to learn
the secrets of your quick bag
You slip into downtown
through underground canals
and surface in the crowd
to pick the prize
to strike the star
and disappear
And in the evening
now that summer comes
the bag of reefer
six-pack of "Private Stock"
and then cocaine
to take you past
Past the corridor
where you piss
the lid the lock the box
past your no name hunger
the dry
of same-same laughter
past fire
past water
past mama
past fourteen

News Item:

The city of Hartford, Connecticut announces a plan
to fence in the Black and Latin communities
in order to "control crime."

winter morning
the moon sits thin
a crooked fading piece of ice on blue
and the sunrise over the projects
catches something new
and the sunrise
over the projects
catches something new
and eight foot
silver painted
chain link
fence
the long gray glint
of rifle muzzles
a cop
on every roof
the search comes door to door
they use their sticks
we leave
milk boiling
eggs burning
diapers unchanged
and are hurried down
to stand in front of the buildings

These will be the rules from today:

1. All residents of this complex will be issued a photo ID which they are to carry at all times. Violation of this regulation will be grounds for immediate confinement.
2. All residents of this complex are to enter and leave only through the checkpoint which has been set up on Parker St. for that purpose.
3. Only those residents with proper working papers may leave the Mission Hill complex.
4. All books, weapons, televisions, radios, record players, musical instruments and drums are to be turned in to the authorities for safe keeping.
5. Curfew shall be at sunset and lights out two hours thereafter. On Saturdays and during the summer lights out shall be three hours after sunset.
6. Remember, these rules are for your protection. The smooth operation of this institution is in everyone's interest.

the paddy wagons
roll in silent
their strobe eyes
flashing
their mouths
wide open
and junior in his pyjamas
breaks
and makes a run for the street
they follow him slowly
and junior in his pyjamas
breaks
and makes a run crying
they follow him slowly from the roofs
so many shots
explode
we cannot

count
and junior in his pyjamas
shatters
hanging in mid air

I am awake
outside in the project night
a nigger had shot a spic
And that was all

America is a Junkie

Old ladies talk to themselves on subways
old ladies smile and talk of death
on long tubes rattling through darkness
on long tubes rattling through dampness
where there is no rain

In the park
cripples chase the winter sun
on canvas wheelchairs
and spit knife looks
at passersby

Between the art museum and the state college
the pickpocket has her sighted
Old lady talks of death and smiles
on long tube rattling
The hand
the hand beneath the coat
the hand moves slowly
the hand
the heart
the hand gropes sweating
for what two or three dollars
won't cop
tonight

In the projects
the ceilings are leaking
We watch the walls dissolve
before our eyes
They are ripping the copper
from our roofs

so the government can buy it back
to mint more pennies

Two police cars
and an ambulance

America is a junkie

Two police cars and an ambulance
America is a junkie

America
is a junkie
flying to the hospital
to be pronounced
Dead on Arrival

For Langston Hughes

On the street in the afternoon
I saw life laughing out the window
of a burnt out room

Bluesman

Bluesman of the broken window
Where is the path
the chain
of events that set you here
Your round face
framed in shredded curtain
your years
like the muffled and cutting sounds
edges of your guitar escaping
While outside
it is late
and crickets sing
the last of summer in a deaf land

Rain

Melody of gutted apartments
a woman's drugged eyes
like dry breasts hanging
in a broken window
Children cry all day
children with empty bellies eating paint
Men that never cry
men with empty bellies carry knives
Teenage girls emptying
their bellies

Que llueva
que llueva
la Virgen de la Cueva

And we of silent parents
who counted all the stars
in the flag at the airport
Children of the crushed dream
who fill our chests with fire
and fill our veins with ice
to walk the street
with faces set in steel
one foot on fear
the other on dry bones
Hang on
like ants on a roller coaster
Hang on
like winos clinging
to the subway gates in winter
for one more breath of warm

Que llueva . . .: children's song calling rain.

Que llueva
que llueva
la Virgen de la Cueva

Odilia is the thin woman
who steered the plow
and broke the hard dirt
of her lame father's land
Bean farmers all
with little to divide
among the brothers and sisters
of the wiry woman with eleven children
She fled to the cold
With a coughing child
and no birth certificates for three
She fled to the cold
Where they don't pay you
to have children
and the billboard
under the window sings
"In Puerto Rico
we make you feel at home
We make you feel at home
in Puerto Rico"

Que llueva
que llueva
la Virgen de la Cueva

Isla del Caribe
faces laughing like maracas
in the round voice of the bomba

bomba: national rhythm of Puerto Rico.

33

Isla del Caribe
the rainbow fruit of your tropics
chained far from the sun
in would be buildings
where life and death
share the same bed

Seven drummers on the front stoop
throw merengue at the sky and laugh
Copper green clouds
tear their hearts on skyscrapers
and water
water
water
is going to fall

merengue: Dominican dance rhythm—lively and very popular.

Cornell Roosevelt Thomas

Born January 28, 1954   Died February 9, 1972

Cornell Roosevelt Thomas
eighteen years old
of forty-one Hollander Street
Dorchester Mass.
Killed
by one black juvenile officer
when stopped for driving his van
the wrong way
on a one way street
Norwell Street, Dorchester Mass.

He was the father
of Cornisia Lavelle Thomas
born May 17, 1972
God has returned the blood

Brujería

It was madness
brujería
She puked
windless hot night
white powder
avocado eye paint
She screamed cement music
sick men's semen
on slick dance floors

It was madness
brujería
and before she knew
it was death
she was singing
She felt the scales
peel off
her third hand steel
tender breasts
and she was moving
In cool water between her thighs
she could taste the salt
in her tears

It was madness
she ran into the mountain
on a moonless night
and was last seen
laughing
in the heart of a mango seed
Brujería

brujería: sorcery.

Project Lovesong

We met
in the city
on a blank street
where life is flat
and squeals
like a rat
on the traintrack

Or did we meet
in the wide yellow moonrise
of an island beach
Bare shoulders
and wet thighs
of you
wide windless moon
And we
locked
seeds in maraca
in the eye of night

We met
in a four walled room
in the gut of a housing project
on a narrow bed
that was always
wide enough
for both

Some Call it Home

there is a weight between my eyes
my mother said
where are we
I did not know
what time is it
I could not tell

the clocks
    bite
the clocks
    spit
people jerk
like rat
like mole
chew their way
through calendar days
that like dirt
some wet
some dry
don't change

it has been determined
that you shall learn
to talk
boy
like them
look
like them
work
for them
it has been determined
that you shall learn

to sell boy
5 10 20
you sell
me sell
young
they are trained
to sell themselves
old
they die stiff
smiling six months of winter
leave the market
in a perfumed box

(but our place of birth
is a pearl among islands
but our patron
a soft brown woman
who pulls
struggling men from the sea)

there is a weight
my mother
between my eyes
a weight not stone
America
some call it home

Five Songs for Puerto Rico

People stare through knot holes
at each other
and each other's fate
Puerto Rico me encanta
pero el welfare me aguanta
says the wall
Behind it a rooster crows
but his sun is strained
through shade and double curtain
He never sees the sky

And the island
is so far away

Death seems to be
the only link
Return for-the-funeral
Return with-the-body
Return as-the-body

And the difference in us
is the difference in the pasteles
the old lady makes
Wrapped in aluminum
they just don't taste the same

2

This woman
born of a wooden house
in the thick of the mountain

40

Among mangó and tamarindo
Near the beginnings of a stream
Where banana is green, fat
and oranges sweet
Journeyed
To live among splinters
To the asthma of the laundry
and a six dollar coat for winter
Three children
in the nights of silence and sirens
three children
to be raised in the smoke of incinerators
three children then four
And the social worker
wants to know
if she
owns boats
or
trailers

This woman's dreams
swallowed a bottle of bleach
and her eyes scream for the island

3

And this man
born where the river meets the sea
where dignity is the child of pain
Son of current and crosscurrent
Of the deep bomba drum
Of calloused canefield hands
and the sweat they poured into the land

This wrestler
tossed up on the streets of six cities
Factory to factory drifter
sometime mason, machinist
check tied to car payments
now unemployed
This juggler of women
is juggled himself:
Sticks and bottles
boricua
Nine white faces
jumped him in the snow
And his skin sighs
for the island

4

The island is not far away
Her palm trees
never took the plane
But someone knocked them down
while you were away

The island is not far away
But her soil is owned by strangers
and governed by parrots
But her flag is wrapped
in thirteen chains
and fifty locks
The island is not far away
But her children are
gone
scattered echoes of her sun

The island wants their hands
The hands that rake the parks
of northern cities
that drive drills for two-thirty-five an hour
and stitch clothes for even less
These laundry hands
the janitor, welder
tobacco picker's hands
The hands
that pound
the wall
and don't know why
they bleed
The island wants these hands

5

This man, this woman
have a daughter
Her mother carried to the island
in the womb
To be born of the mountain
and the trees
Of the river, sea and deep
drum
And she too journeyed
Journeyed before she knew
To greet this grave
this arbitrary madness
this number that never hits
At four
she whispers Puerto Rico
At twenty
she will scream

A güiro is silence
without quick hands to play it
The island needs
her daughter's song

güiro: a dried gourd, hollow, with scratches cut into it. A percussion instrument.

44

Abuela y Patria

Vino en el avión con los ojos cerrados
Abuela de cuarenta
nietos ausentes
Madre de una campesina
un estudiante, un preso
¡Qué lejos las lomas secas de Ponce!
las talas de gandules
los aguaceros de octubre . . .
El pelo lo lleva en un moño
suelto le toca las rodillas—
con canas y risas
te envuelve en su cuento
Ella tose
tú maldices la ventana rota
Yo te miro a ti y la miro a ella
Sube el invierno
pero no hay vela que apague

No olvides, boricua,
cuando el viento raspe
los proyectos
con lengua de alambre
que tu patria es una india cautiva
¿y tú?
Semilla dormida

Tiempo Muerto

Batata and rice
or rice alone
or fish if there was fish
sweet potato and fish

Nothing shook my grandmother's house
Water that ran in the river
left the banks unchanged

Lloréns Torres to New York
came in July looking for snowflakes
Trained as a welder in Newark
no welders wanted
Tobacco in Hartford
Apples on Route 202
Vagrant in Greenfield
winter in Springfield
food stamps in Boston

Batata and rice
or rice alone
or fish if there was fish
sweet potato and fish

Run
grandmother
run
River's in flood
animals bloated and drowned

Tiempo Muerto: lit. "dead time." The five months of the year that canecutters
spent unemployed.
Lloréns Torres: housing project in San Juan.

The late noon high
comes and goes
Beer is still cheaper
than wine
Found no work
spent the day
burning gasoline

Aguacero

Dark dirt flees
Sudden walls of cold drops
sting palms
strike red from flamboyan
swallow the singing of birds
To make the best of it
grandmother pushes you out
slipping
shivering with cake of white soap
The rain falls
in mambo pattern
filling the bucket
splashing the thighs
of country girls

Songs for Puerto Rico #2

Cradle of the evening
this soft sloping crescent
brown valley of hidden roads
Old men with machetes
thin as the mist
silent as rock
climb the curves
Here the morning
hear the mockingbird
here the carved stone of the indian

My house is on a hill
compadre
where no one can reach
My house is on a hill
compadre
I fetch my own water
I burn my own light
I'm with the hawk
when he makes a kill
I watch the city
in the distance boiling
with blue and white teeth

EL YUNQUE

The mountain
The anvil crushes clouds

El Yunque: lit. "the anvil." Puerto Rico's tallest peak, the rain forest home of
Yukiyú.

Yellow streams
uproot jungle trees
and shatter on smooth stones
Flashes of orchid
life is green
and thick as the air
Hibiscus bushes
yellow and red
Dripping leaves loaded with snails
Quick lizards
disappearing

Five hundred years ago
in a time before paved roads
our streams ran clean
to Luquillo's clear beach
We kept the balance then
and demanded little
of men
Five hundred years
and what can you show
but a people torn
as this red earth
You say we are dead
but what can you show
You say we are dead
You can't see us
but do you see yourself

And you come to the mountain
encased in air-conditioned cars
you do not wish to breathe the air
you must not take home dirty shoes
Take motion pictures instead

they save trips back
Strangers to your own land
you will not leave the path
you will not reach the peak
you will not find the clearing
where unseen birds
from unseen branches scream
Yukiyú
though all seems still

BACK AWAY

Two days after I returned
her children were running
in the project lot
Their smiles outshone
the broken glass
I could see them
in Loiza
deep in the palms
cracking cocos
and selling crabs

Yukiyú: protector of the tainos; his home is El Yunque.
Loiza: town on the north coast of Puerto Rico. Famous for its people, its music,
its food.

Canto Popular

A Matanzas voy
caballero,
a tocar
la rumba que vino primero
A Matanzas, voy a Matanzas
A Matanzas, voy a Matanzas . . .

Tela de vidrio roto
que tapa mis días
Camino entre las ruinas
en la calle agua sucia
puertas que abren
a paredes garabateadas
un par que otro
de ojos asustados
envueltos en sus cortinas

Esta es la tierra
a la que llegamos
Soñador, el sueño te salió pesado
y por no volverte loco
te amarraste al yugo
y aceptaste la rutina
Y te estrangulan en la nieve
hoy, mañana, cada día

No hay más remedio que olvidar
            —dicen algunos—
ponerle nombre americano a los hijos
saludar a tus hermanos en inglés
(para que sepan que yo sí sé)
I am proud

to be a
bueno, no sé qué
Pero la cuestión es
que hay que vivir la vida
lucir la facha de hoy
do the hustle
and with a lovely smile
dejarse sepultar

¿Y si fruto de mamey
es mi tierra,
jugo de sol
que chupo en los campos de mi memoria?
Me abrigo la sangre con ella
¿Y si cuando mis manos vuelan
sobre el cuero del tambor
sigo los pasos de los bisabuelos
digo su nombre
y como en filo de machete
corre mi voz?

Hay pueblos que desaparecen
Se duermen en la avenida de acero
y nunca más se sienten cantar

Hay pueblos que salen del invierno
como el águila cuando sube al cielo
la serpiente entre sus garras

Y hay pueblos
que llevan a sus hijos de la mano
hasta donde se puede ver muy lejos
y dicen
Ahí está el mañana

anda
corre
yo te sigo
Mira que bonito sería
    mi china
Oye que bonito sería
    mi china

Afro Blue

for Mongo

one long note . . .

glass
cutting glass
cutting
young woman's skin
blood
gone brittle
in an old man's leg

One long note . . .

the moon is hunting
tonight her razors
scream
across the land
the moon is hunting
tonight
the moon will eat

One long note . . .

sweeter
than mango is sweet
warmer

Song of the Drum

for Les Wood

"Elemental
united in vision"
Carved into this shape
a piece of my home

The drum has survived
thick womb
outlawed
is filling again
in mystery
in hardness
Few hands can speak
but the drum has survived
competing with sirens for air
to issue its call

And we answer
(let's face it
we have not done so well)
with wine bottle
for a cowbell
pills in a box
to shake
Here to argue
fight and leave
tripping
on our way
Who spits in the air
dirties only his own face

"Elemental, united in vision": Christopher Okigbo, *Labyrinths*.

56

The drum
free of the thin
white lines that divide us
The drum has survived
The shattered thread of years
can be taken up in rhythm
The drum is time
One man bought fifty years
another twenty-four
uncle took eighty
but who can take it all
The drummer's gone
he left his drum alone

who holds the key
we call on you
who holds the key
we call on you
the path is there
for those who walk
in 6/8 time
we call on you
guaguancó coro miyare
let it be heard
guaguancó coro miyare
in the stars and on the earth
guaguancó coro miyare
across a sea beyond memory
Chola came walking back
oido   (*sung*)
Chola came walking back
Silencio   (*sung*)

oido: listen.   *silencio:* silence.

Rumba

Left La Habana . . .
The guaguancó
went for a trip
The guaguancó
got to the moon
The guaguancó was hot
but found no palm to shade
The guaguancó had thirst
but found no rum to drink
The guaguancó raised up
before the astronauts came
The guaguancó went back to Cuba
The guaguancó
sounds just the same
Throw down your crutch
said the drum to the cripple
it's time to play
my game

2

Rumba earth and rumba cloud
The skin is tight and mute
the body round
and heavy
This rhythm is a queen
who has no masters
and no death

rumba: mother of Cuban rhythms.

Drummers come and drummers go
and rumba remains the same

You must
move softly
There are no doors
That you can knock down
to enter
You will sweat
You will tire
You will split your hands
in patterns your father never learned

where the sun rises
donde sale el sol
where the sun rises
nació la rumba
where the sun rises
rumba was born
donde sale el sol

Like a fruit
you tasted in childhood
you will taste it again
and know its name

3

Quinto growls
and explodes
We strain to hold

quinto: top drum. It speaks or "solos," over the rumba.

The swaying rumba speaks:

Time eats the father's father
and the father's children
Death blows
and the strongest fly
like leaves
We salute you
we have seen you fall
and rise
and fall
The feet are the support of the body
our feet move slowly from afar
We salute you

Fire was our tongue
the heat of birth
We would offer you mango then
and say
look
This is our life
We too
grow from the soil
and when we pass
leave our seed
to root
that it may bear fruit
in the sun

Fire is our tongue
The ashes
of memory singed
with branding iron
Our stunted seed

Chains calling
from the bottom of the sea
give us no rest
Canefields scream
and we burn
and birth is cold
and heat belongs to fever

We salute you

And we must wrap ourselves
in the thin cloth
in the worn cloth of patience
we who are hungry
and wait for our dawn
to be fed

4

When they heard the drum
was still alive
they could not explain
"We thought the climate
the atmosphere did not lend . . ."
They sent a mission
to investigate
research
One brought a sound recorder
the other
measuring tape
They wanted definitions
"Excuse me please
how do you spell . . ."

But he could not be reached for comment
The drummer was far away
He had hitched his quinto
to south bound rumba
and had taken off
on the up
beat

Changó/Thunder

Changó
we brought you here on our backs
Where the Pilgrims lie
now stands Changó
The Pilgrims are dead, Changó
Changó
we brought your here on our backs

Changó laughs
Changó laughs
I laugh
with the fire
of red pearl
Changó laughs

moon boils
sky winces
palms overrun
the city wailing
mango tree wrestles
mirror tower
a thousand congas leap
Thunder
canesweet on the El tracks

Changó
Changó
Ya rompió
Kaguo
Kabiosile ó

Changó: Yoruba god of thunder.

Rumba Fragments

Onto the barrel
that once held rum
took fish in salt
across the sea
you tack the skin
the owner owned
before the mule
took sick
And the circle
is complete
tightened with fire
ready to receive
the heat of hands

Look
laughing on the crown of that tree:
Windbeaten king of swaying palm
let me slice this rumba
so you can eat
let me pour this rumba
The earth drinks rum
your feet
her hips
drink drum
before the bleeding eye
of the morning sun

We brought no books, you see
no armies
no historians with greedy pens

Windbeaten king . . .: Changó.

Only memory
Remembered patterns
the hands mold into song
A cry at starfall:
rumba
take us in your beak
to rise
hawk height
and slip the people
whose hands can't fly

call the rumba
call the drummer
dawn is home
call the rumba
his hands/flying stones
call the drummer
black birds rising/yellow sky
call the rumba
coconut meat is white
call the drummer
he has
gaps in his teeth
who has
gaps in his teeth
he has
gaps in his teeth
gaps in his teeth
like a
hunched over   crocodile
            smiling

Dance of the Ancestors

1/1/76

The mask dancing has no joints

Seed silent
burnt womb
of wood
chewing time

The mask dancing has no joints

Its face flying
its belly
falls

The mask dancing has no joints

Thunder
on a thread

The mask dancing has no joints

The truth kills
like an arrow

The mask dancing has no joints

Men
steal the land
but the land eats
men

The mask dancing has no joints

The stick that killed a black dog yesterday
kills a white dog
tomorrow

The mask dancing has no joints

The goat that
breaks
the drumskin
with his own
hide
must pay

The mask dancing has no joints

The wind does
as he pleases
man/woman can
you put
him
in chains

The mask dancing has no joints

Who
has
no
heart does
not go
to
war

The mask dancing has no joints

And I go to war

. . .

Five hundred years ago today
we fled our home in flames
our dead littered
the crossroads
Children
drank from needles

Cimarrón

for Esteban Montejo

What an old man
can see sitting down
a young man
can't see
standing up
young men
must climb hills
in winter
hear me

The chain is tightest
when the links are weakest

On the skin of the slave
the master burnt his name
The overseer
spat
on the wound
to cool it
The slave disappeared
He planted his feet
in the forest night
Where moon, wind and cold wrestle
he went to wrestle too
He spoke to no one
for ten years
the stream spoke to him

Cimarrón: runaway slave.
"What an old man can see sitting down": Ibo Proverb.

From his cave in the day
he heard the howling
of the master's dogs

Under the turban of night
(He saw no one for ten years)
Under the turban of night
he came down
with a stolen machete
sharp as the crescent moon
Now a mockingbird sings
in the master's skull

Hear me

There are no masters
There are no slaves

Morning Coming

1

You have to stumble
before you can walk
and we played hopscotch
before we shot dope
And our parents stroked our hair
and blessed us
with hand-me-down dreams
Smile together
for Easter Sunday pictures
and go on
crumbling
hollow walls
of empty eyed buildings

And my story is not young
I'm told
It happened years ago
We spoke less english then
but took the same fall
You have to stumble
before you can walk

2

And the lines keep growing . . .

Comay Marta and Comay Luz
embracing after seven years
in line en la oficina del welfare
for apartamento and furnitura
estampillas and a special dieta

para diabetis
del corazon

Methadone clinic
Jelly silence for half a block
The sun
just beginning to sweat
the junkies
just beginning to shake

You wanna go out
you have to wait inside the door
There are scars on her legs
but she's thirteen
believe me mister
even though she looks
fifteen

3

Search
And what will you find here
you cannot
walk to the sea in the evening
and say:
Wash me
There are no mockingbird mornings
No hills of heat and milk
No forest
no shadow to strike from

Flamboyan leaves
hurricane blown
long gone

Our blossoms don't glow
Our stems will not grow

4

Me voy pa La Habana
a divertirme
a bailar merengue
que quiero morirme . . .
Return
Put it in a blue note
But return
a stranger who must learn
to chew the food again
Put it in a blue note
You have to wander
before you can rest
Put it in a blue note
They say
you have to harden
in the fire of the pavements
Put it in a blue note
The tropical sun is years away
Put it in a blue note
The dream you want to
crack open like a coconut
Put it in a blue note
And you thirsty for milk
a bailar merengue
A bailar
A bailar merengue
A gozar . . .

Me voy pa La Habana: "I'm going to Havana"–song.

5

Our grandfathers
were new children
who won the islands
when they dropped their chains
and took the hills
You have to stumble
before you can walk

And we have been
pounced on
On all these streets twisted
beaten
tied
and still dreaming
sold
And falling we must stumble
and stumbling we must walk
and walking we must learn
learn to sting
little man be a scorpion
for who can hold a scorpion
in his fist
little man
who can hold a scorpion
in his fist

6

When the morning comes
in gleaming wail of liquid horn
When the morning comes
frozen in blue note song
When the morning comes

grasping in 6/8 time
When the morning comes
When the morning comes
When the morning comes
To our hills of cement
I will be there
blind
riding the teeth of a samba
snaking up the street

DEMCO